TOP TIPS

Be the Best at Science

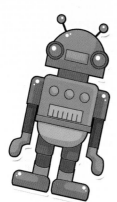

Rebecca Rissman

www.raintreepublishers.co.uk
Visit our website to find out
more information about
Raintree books.

To order:
☎ Phone 0845 6044371
📠 Fax +44 (0) 1865 312263
💻 Email myorders@raintreepublishers.co.uk

Customers from outside the UK please telephone +44 1865 312262

Raintree is an imprint of Capstone Global Library
Limited, a company incorporated in England and
Wales having its registered office at 7 Pilgrim Street,
London, EC4V 6LB – Registered company number:
6695582

Text © Capstone Global Library Limited 2013
First published in hardback in 2013
First published in paperback in 2014
The moral rights of the proprietor have been
asserted.

Edited by Rebecca Rissman, Dan Nunn, and
 Adrian Vigliano
Designed by Joanna Hinton-Malivoire
Original illustrations © Capstone Global Library Ltd
Picture research by Ruth Blair
Originated by Capstone Global Library
Printed in China by CTPS

ISBN 978 1 406 24107 5 (hardback)
16 15 14 13 12
10 9 8 7 6 5 4 3 2 1

ISBN 978 1 406 24112 9 (paperback)
17 16 15 14 13
10 9 8 7 6 5 4 3 2 1

British Library Cataloguing in Publication Data
A full catalogue record for this book is available
from the British Library.

Acknowledgements
The author and publishers are grateful to the
following for permission to reproduce copyright
material: Shutterstock pp. 5 (© Mat Hayward),
7 (© wavebreakmedia ltd), 9 (© James Steidl),
11 (© Skripko Ievgen), 13 (© Tspider), 15 (©
Dmitriy Shironosov), 17 (© taelove7), 17 (© Scott
Sanders), 18 (© darkgreenwolf), 19 (© Yurchyks),
19 (© darkgreenwolf), 19 (© Ilya Andriyanov),
21 (© Glenda M. Powers), 23 (© Cheryl Casey),
24 (© Monkey Business Images), 27 (© oorka),
29 (© Symbiot), 30 (© Carlos E. Santa Maria).
Background and design features reproduced with
the permission of Shutterstock.

Cover photograph reproduced with the permission
of Shutterstock and Shutterstock/© notkoo.

We would like to thank Nancy Harris for her
invaluable help in the preparation of this book.

Every effort has been made to contact copyright
holders of any material reproduced in this book.
Any omissions will be rectified in subsequent
printings if notice is given to the publisher.

Some words are shown in bold, like this. You can find
out what they mean by looking in the glossary.

Contents

Get going!

People use science every day to do all kinds of things. But sometimes science can seem tricky. Don't let that stop you! Learning a few simple tricks can make even the biggest science **experiment** more fun!

Top Tip

Get going! The more science you do, the easier it will get. Spend 15 minutes every day asking scientific questions. Try to do scientific experiments, too!

Use the scientific method

We use a set of steps called the **scientific method** to answer questions or solve problems in science. Using the scientific method makes sure that the answer, or **outcome**, of an **experiment** is something you can trust.

Question	ask what you would like to know about a topic
Observe	learn what you can about your topic
Hypothesize	make an informed guess about the answer to your question
Experiment	test your hypothesis or guess
Record data	take notes on what happens
Draw a conclusion	decide whether your hypothesis was correct

Don't miss a step!

The **scientific method** is very helpful to scientists. But you need to remember all the steps!

Top Tip

Memorise this: "Queens Only Have Expensive Royal Dinners".

8

Test that tip!

Each word in the sentence starts with the first letter of the words in the scientific method:

Queens: **Question**

Only: **Observe**

Have: **Hypothesize**

Expensive: **Experiment**

Royal: **Record data**

Dinners: **Draw a conclusion**

Question this!

Asking the right type of questions is very important in science.

You should be able to test your question by changing one **variable**, or thing, to find your answer. Only ask questions that require one change in your **experiment**, or test.

Got it!

Test that tip!

You wonder how long it would take someone to cycle 1 kilometre. Which question works better?

How long does it take to cycle 1 kilometre? OR

How long does it take Julia to ride her bicycle for 1 kilometre?

Observe it!

The second step of the **scientific method** reminds us to **observe**, or look closely at, our topic. This might mean doing **research** to learn more about the topic.

Top Tip

When observing your topic, make a KWL chart:

- Things I *know*
- Things I *want* to know
- Things I've *learned*

Bikes

Things I *know*	
Things I *want* to know	
Things I've *learned*	

Make a guess!

After you have **observed** your topic, it's time to make your **hypothesis**, or best guess. For example, "If Julia rides her bike downhill, then her speed will increase" is a hypothesis. Remember, it doesn't matter if your hypothesis is right or wrong. The results of your experiment will still be valuable!

Top Tip
Many good hypotheses fit into the "If, Then" pattern.

Wheeee!

Test that tip!

Can you make your hypothesis fit into this pattern?
If [this happens], then [this] will happen.

Pay attention!

While you do your science **experiment**, or test, remember to pay attention. You will need to take notes and look at everything that happens. If you don't **record**, or write down your results, no one will know what you were able to prove!

Top Tip

Pay attention to **details** when you take notes. Always:

- Record the date of your experiment.
- Write down any measurements you take.
- Record the materials you use.
- If possible, take photos.

14 December

It takes 30 seconds for Julia to ride from the kerb to the tree.

Measure it!

Science **experiments**, or tests, often ask you to measure different things. You need to remember which tools are used for which measurements!

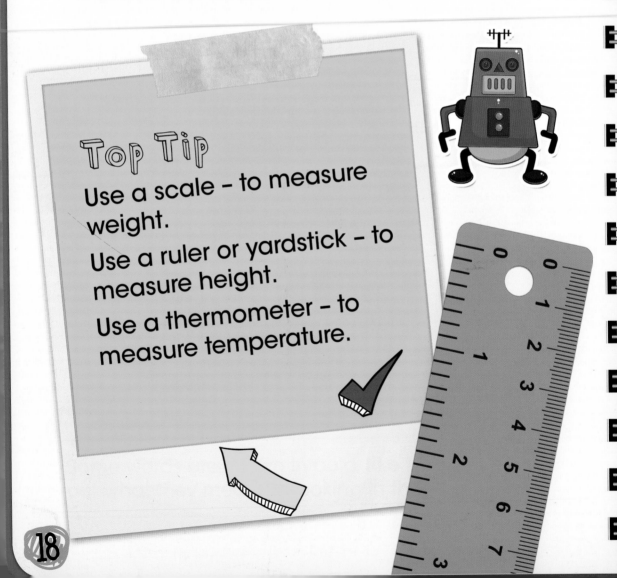

Top Tip

Use a scale – to measure weight.

Use a ruler or yardstick – to measure height.

Use a thermometer – to measure temperature.

Test that tip!

What tool would you use to measure the width of a bicycle tyre?

Keeping count

Some **experiments**, or tests, have results that you can count or measure. When doing this type of experiment, remember to **record**, or write down all your results.

Top Tip

When writing your notes, remind yourself to record measurements by asking "Can We Try?"

Test that tip!

Each word in the question starts with the first letter of different measuring words.

Can: Count

We: Weigh

Try: Time how long something takes

Get the picture!

Some **experiments**, or tests, do not have results that you can count or measure. For example, the following **hypothesis** cannot be measured in numbers: "If Julia exercises before she rides her bike, then her face turns red." To **record** what happens in these experiments, you need to:

- Draw a picture.
- Take a photograph.
- Write a description.

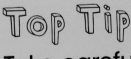

Top Tip

Take careful notes!

Test that tip!

Which is a better description of the outcome of this experiment: Julia's nose and forehead were pink, and her cheeks turned dark red.

OR

Her face was red.

Phew...

Draw a conclusion

Your conclusion is a summary of how your **experiment** results either showed that your hypothesis was correct or incorrect.

Don't worry if your experiment didn't prove your hypothesis! It still helped you to learn something!

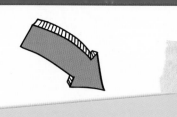

Top Tip

Don't forget to share your results! There are many fun ways to teach others what you've learned, such as:

A video

A school report

A science poster

Using mnemonics

Science teaches us amazing things about the world around us. But sometimes there can be a lot to remember. **Mnemonics** are tools we can use to remember things. Page 8 of this book uses a mnemonic to remember the steps in the **scientific method**.

"Queens Only Have Expensive Royal Dinners".

Top Tip

Make your own mnemonics as you study science!

Test that tip!
Write a mnemonic to help you remember the names of the eight planets in our solar system.

Study like a pro!

Set yourself up to succeed by practising these tips when you study or do your homework.

Top Tip

Before you get to work, always:

➡ Eat a healthy snack

➡ Turn off the television

➡ Make sure you have all the supplies you need:

- textbook
- scrap paper
- pencils and rubber

Dream big!

Remember, learning science can be useful in many ways as you grow up! You can use it to ask questions and learn more about the world. Or you might use it in your job as a teacher, doctor, or pilot!

Glossary

data information collected, such as facts, statistics, or observations

detail small part

experiment controlled test to learn something

hypothesize (hypothesis) educated guess about the outcome of an experiment

mnemonic interesting or fun way to remember something

observe to carefully watch or notice

outcome final product or end result

record write down

research careful investigation into something

scientific method way to do an experiment. The scientific method has six steps.

variable part of a scientific experiment that can change

Find out more

Books

Investigations and Inventions (Sci-Hi series), Andrew Solway (Raintree, 2010)

My Science Investigation (series), Christine Taylor-Butler (Raintree, 2012)

Websites

www.bbc.co.uk/schools/ks2bitesize/science
Visit the BBC Bitesize Science website for help and advice with all your science subjects, plus interactive games, quizzes, and lots of other activities.

www.sciencebob.com/sciencefair/ideas.php
Having trouble thinking of a topic for an experiment? Try this great website for ideas!

Index